Against the World

I Figured It Out:

One Father's Journey of Love, Resilience, and Family

Dedication

To my children and family.

By Martin Mesa

FOREWORD

This book began as a story I carried quietly for many years.

It began in a small campo in the Dominican Republic called Cuenda, where life was simple, hard, and full of love. We didn't have electricity or running water, but we had family, community, and the kind of strength that grows out of necessity.

I came to the United States at nine years old, not knowing the language, not knowing what life would demand of me. I only knew that we were leaving everything familiar behind, and that somehow, we had to begin again.

Since then, life has asked me to restart more than once.

I have been a son, an immigrant, a young father, a single dad, a man rebuilding his career from nothing, and above all, a father of four children who gave my life meaning beyond myself.

This memoir is written first for my children — Carina, Martin Jr., Katie, and Mateo.

So that one day, no matter where life takes you, you will always know where you come from. You will always know how deeply you are loved. You were never a burden. You were my purpose.

And this book is also for anyone reading who feels overwhelmed, who feels behind, who feels like life has taken more than it has given.

This is proof that hardship does not have to be the end of the story.

Hope is not something you wait for.

Hope is something you choose.

Again, and again.

Author's Note

This book is a memoir.

Every story in these pages is rooted in my real life — in the places that raised me, the people who shaped me, and the moments that tested me.

Some details have been simplified for clarity, but the heart of the story is true.

I didn't write this because my life was perfect.

I wrote it because it was real.

I wrote it because so many people walk through life carrying struggles quietly, wondering if they are the only ones starting over, the only ones trying to figure it out.

I want my children to know that their father's life was built through love, sacrifice, and perseverance.

And I want the reader to know that no matter where you begin, no matter how many times life forces you to restart, there is always a path forward.

This is my story.

And if it brings even one person hope, then it was worth telling.

Chapter 1 — Cuenda Mornings

In Cuenda, mornings didn't begin with alarms.

They began with light.

Not electric light — we didn't have that — but the slow natural light of the Dominican sun rising over the campo, spilling warmth into a world that was already awake. Roosters called out before anyone spoke. The air carried the smell of earth and distance, like the land itself was breathing.

By the time I was a child, work was already part of life's rhythm. Not as punishment. Not as something to complain about. Just as reality.

I was born the youngest of fifteen children — the baby, the pequeño — and even though many of my older brothers and sisters had already married or left for other cities, the sense of family was never small. Family wasn't something around me — it was the foundation I lived inside.

Although I was the youngest, the household itself often felt smaller. Many of my older brothers and sisters had already married or moved away by the time I was growing up. Still, I have always been close to my siblings. I come from a family that stays connected, and I consider my nieces and nephews as my own. Even now, my family remains my rock.

My parents are my anchors. I still go to them for advice, for wisdom, and sometimes just for the simple comfort of conversation. Their love shaped me long before I understood what love really meant.

We were poor.

No electricity. No running water. No luxuries.

Nights were truly dark. Mornings began early. Work was never optional. From a young age, I learned that life didn't hand anything to you — it had to be earned. My parents carried burdens with quiet strength, and that became my blueprint: responsibility before comfort, effort before excuses.

Some of my earliest memories are not of big events, but of routines — the kind of routines that teach you life without ever announcing themselves.

I remember walking to school as a little boy with my sister Christina and a group of kids our age. School wasn't close. We walked almost three miles. With notebooks in our hands, we followed the dirt road that stretched ahead of us until we reached a simple wooden structure that served as our classroom.

At noon, dismissal came quickly.

And then... the walk back.

The sun was higher. The road felt longer. Hunger began to speak.

When I arrived home, I often found my mother already prepared for the next responsibility, as if she had been waiting not for rest but for the next task.

She would have food packed — not small portions — but enough for my father and the workers in the field. A full casserole of beans. A pot of rice. Enough for men working under the heat all day.

My task was always the same: I would accompany her, carrying the gallon of fresh water behind her.

I can still see myself walking a few steps behind my mom, small and trying my best to keep up. Sometimes I fell behind. Sometimes by the time I reached the field, they had already started eating.

The workers would laugh when they saw me.

They would tease me.

"¡Mira el chiquito, siempre lento!"

Look at the little one, always slow.

And I felt the heat of embarrassment, the childish frustration of wanting to be faster, stronger, older.

But I was just a boy.

A boy trying his best.

My father would look up, serious, strong character in his eyes — when he spoke, you listened — but there was always softness beneath it. He didn't say much. He didn't need to.

His presence was enough.

When it was time to return home, the day still wasn't finished.

Later, I would go with my older brothers to the river to bring the horses to drink water. That task felt different. It was still responsibility, but it carried joy inside it.

The river was freedom.

The horses bending their heads to drink. The sound of water moving. The sunlight reflecting like something holy.

We laughed.

It felt like going to the beach on a sunny day, even though it was just another part of survival.

That was childhood in Cuenda.

Long walks.

Heavy water.

Work disguised as routine.

Joy hiding inside simple things.

And even now, if someone asked me if I would change it...

I wouldn't.

Because it made me.

Because it taught me early that life is carried one step at a time.

Chapter 2 — The Only Television in Town

In Cuenda, nighttime was different.

When the sun went down, the world didn't just get darker.

It got quieter.

There were no streetlights. No glowing windows across the neighborhood. Darkness came naturally, wrapping the campo in a silence that felt ancient, like the same silence that had existed long before us.

Inside our small wooden home, the night belonged to routine.

My parents would sit together with a small battery-operated radio, listening to the news. That radio was our connection to everything beyond Cuenda — beyond San Juan, beyond the Dominican Republic, beyond the life we knew.

And while they listened...

my siblings and I would feel something else pulling at us.

Because in our town, there was one place at night where people gathered.

My godfather's house.

He owned the only television around.

Somehow, he powered it with a car battery.

At night, neighbors would fill his small living room, shoulder to shoulder. Children sat on the floor. Adults stood behind them. Everyone quieted when the screen came alive.

Telenovelas.

Dramatic music.

Stories of love and heartbreak that felt far from our lives, yet belonged to us all the same.

People laughed together, gasped together, shouted at the characters as if they could hear.

For those hours, poverty disappeared.

Not because it was gone...

but because joy filled the space.

Happiness doesn't require abundance.

Happiness requires connection.

When the show ended, people spilled back into the darkness, still talking, still smiling.

Those nights taught me something I didn't understand until much later:

Even in struggle, life contains beauty.

Chapter 3 — The Day the House Burned

One of the clearest memories of my childhood in Cuenda is not a game, or a walk to school, or even the river.

It is fire.

I was very young — only about five or six years old — small enough to still be carried by fear more than reason.

We lived in a simple wooden house, the kind of house many families lived in back then. There was no fire department nearby, no emergency number to call, no quick rescue if something went wrong.

Life in the campo was beautiful, but it was also fragile.

I remember it was Three Kings Day, one of the happiest days for a child. My older sister Juana and her husband Alcibiades bought me a small toy horse with a rider on top. It had a little pump, and when you pressed it, the horse would move forward as if it were galloping.

To me, it was everything.

I took it outside to play, proud of this rare gift, excited to show it off.

At some point, I brought it to my cousin. While we were playing, he stepped on it by accident.

One of the horse's legs snapped off.

I froze.

My heart sank.

I picked it up carefully and brought it back home, carrying it like something wounded.

I placed it on the bed and searched for the broken piece. I noticed it had fallen behind the bed, deep into the darkness underneath.

I wanted to see where it went.

Near the bed, my parents kept a small gas lamp. At night, they would light it with matches. I had seen them do it many times.

Without understanding what danger was, I reached for the matches.

I struck one.

The small flame appeared.

I crawled under the bed holding the match, trying to find the toy's missing leg.

And then...

the mattress caught.

At first, it was only a little flame.

Then it grew.

Then it spread.

I panicked.

I ran out from under the bed, terrified, and went straight to my mother.

I didn't even speak.

I couldn't.

My chest was pounding so hard that I thought it might break through my ribs.

My mother touched my chest and asked, *"What have you done that your heart is beating like this?"*

Before I could answer, we heard neighbors shouting outside.

"¡Comadre! Your house is on fire!"

Suddenly, everything became chaos.

The house was wood. The fire moved fast.

There was no fire truck coming down the road.

There were only neighbors, running with buckets of water, throwing dirt, trying desperately to save what they could.

But the flames didn't care.

They consumed everything.

Our home...

our clothes...

our belongings...

everything we owned went up into smoke.

I remember standing there, small and silent, watching grown adults fight a fire they could not control.

I was too scared to speak.

I still did not say it was me.

When my father arrived, his face changed the moment he saw what was left — burned debris, ashes, the remains of our life.

He went for the police. A report was made. People came to investigate.

And still, I stayed quiet.

Until I saw them questioning my mother.

Something inside me cracked.

I thought she was going to get in trouble for what I had done.

And in that moment, I stepped forward.

I told them the truth.

I told them about the toy.

The match.

The accident.

It was the worst feeling I have ever known.

Not because I feared punishment...

but because I saw the pain in my parents' eyes as they looked through what was left.

We were already poor.

And now we had nothing.

That day, I learned something too early:

How quickly life can change.

How fragile everything is.

And how heavy guilt can be, even on the chest of a little boy.

It was a tragedy.

But it was also the beginning of resilience.

Because my parents did what they always did.

They did not fall apart.

They rebuilt.

And without realizing it, they were teaching me the lesson that would follow me my entire life:

When everything burns down...

you start again.

Chapter 4 — Baseball in the Dust

Afternoons in Cuenda belonged to the children.

Mornings were for school, for long walks with notebooks in our hands, for carrying water behind our mothers, for watching the adults work the land as if life depended on it.

Because it did.

But afternoons...

afternoons were different.

The sun still burned high, the air still smelled like earth, but there was a lightness that arrived when the hardest tasks slowed down.

That was when we became kids again.

We played baseball.

Not the organized kind with uniforms and perfect fields.

Ours was baseball made from imagination.

We didn't have equipment the way people do in America.

We didn't have stadiums or gloves for everyone.

Sometimes we didn't even have a real ball.

But we always found a way.

A stick became a bat.

A worn-out ball became treasure.

A patch of open land became our stadium.

We ran through dust, shouting, laughing, arguing over whether someone was safe or out.

There was always someone claiming the call was unfair.

There was always someone swinging too hard.

And there was always joy.

Baseball in Cuenda wasn't just a game.

It was freedom.

It was a world where you weren't poor or rich, farmer's son or teacher's son.

You were just a kid trying to hit the ball.

Trying to run faster than the others.

Trying to win.

Even back then, something about the game pulled me in.

I was short.

The chiquito of the group.

But I wanted it.

I wanted to belong inside that circle of laughter and competition.

Sometimes we played until the light began to fade, until someone's mother called them home, until hunger reminded us that reality was still waiting.

And when we weren't playing baseball, we made our own fun.

We handcrafted little cars with our hands, shaping toys out of almost nothing.

We made kites.

That was one of the greatest joys — building something yourself and watching it rise.

There was something powerful about holding the string, feeling the pull of the wind, watching your kite climb higher into the wide Dominican sky.

It felt like possibility.

Like even a child from Cuenda could lift something into the air.

My father was a man of strong character.

When he spoke, you listened.

He didn't believe in raising lazy men.

He didn't want my older brothers growing up as vagos.

So even when the day slowed down, rest didn't mean idleness.

Sometimes on those quiet afternoons, he would look at my brothers and say:

"Vamos... go fishing. Go catch today's dinner."

Just like that, responsibility became adventure.

My brothers and I would collect worms, walk down to the river, and spend hours fishing.

We waited.

We joked.

We competed quietly.

And when a fish finally pulled, when the line tightened, it felt like victory.

Not just because it meant food...

but because it meant we had done something real.

We had provided.

Even as boys.

Looking back, I realize how much my father was teaching without lectures.

Discipline.

Purpose.

Manhood built through contribution.

But he never stole joy.

Because we loved those moments.

They became memories.

They became part of who we were.

I didn't know then that baseball would follow me.

That the game I played barefoot in Cuenda would one day give me belonging in Brooklyn.

Life has a strange way of planting seeds early.

And baseball was one of mine.

Chapter 5 — Goodbye to the Campo

There are moments in life that divide everything.

Moments so large that you don't fully understand them while they're happening, but later you realize they were the turning point — the line between one life and the next.

For me, that moment came when we left Cuenda.

It began with my father's youngest brother, my Tío Paco.

He had been living in the United States for a long time, far away from the campo, far away from the life my father knew.

He petitioned for my father and our family to come to America.

And petitions are slow.

They take years.

Life continues while you wait.

Children grow.

People marry.

Seasons pass.

Cuenda remains Cuenda.

And then one day, after all that time, the impossible became real.

We were given visas.

But the visas weren't for everyone.

They were only for my parents and for the children under twenty-one.

Which meant...

we had to leave our older brothers and sisters behind.

Some were already married.

Some had already built lives of their own.

But they were still our family.

Migration wasn't just moving.

It was dividing.

As a child, you don't think about immigration law.

You think about faces.

Who is coming with you...

and who is not.

The days leading up to our departure felt unreal.

People came to visit.

Goodbyes began early.

Friends looked at us differently, as if we had already started disappearing.

I was only nine years old.

But I felt something deep in my chest:

I was leaving the only world I knew.

The campo.

The dirt roads.

The river.

The nights in my godfather's house.

The afternoons of baseball in the dust.

The smell of my mother's cooking.

The strength of my father's presence.

Cuenda wasn't just where I lived.

Cuenda was who I was.

And now I was being asked to walk away from it.

We weren't moving from Cuenda to San Juan.

No.

We were moving from Cuenda...

to New York.

The distance wasn't just miles.

It was culture.

Language.

Weather.

Life itself.

I didn't know what America would demand of me.

I only knew that I was going.

A small boy from a campo called Cuenda...

about to step into the largest city I could not even imagine.

And the moment we left, I understood something without words:

Life was beginning again.

Chapter 6 — November 23rd, 1993

Some dates stay with you forever.

Not because someone told you they were important...

but because your body remembers them.

For me, one of those dates is November 23rd, 1993.

That was the day we arrived in New York City.

I was nine years old.

I had left Cuenda behind — the campo, the dirt roads, the river, the life that felt small but complete. And now I was stepping into something enormous, something loud, something unknown.

New York was not a city to a child like me.

It was a world.

I remember the moment we came outside.

The cold hit our faces like a brick hitting glass.

It wasn't just cold.

It was shocking.

In Cuenda, the air was warm and familiar.

In New York, winter greeted us like a warning.

The wind felt sharp, almost aggressive, as if the city itself was saying:

Welcome... but you will have to adapt.

I didn't have the clothes for it.

None of us did.

We were children from the Dominican countryside, dressed for a life that belonged to the sun.

And now the sun felt far away.

All I remember from that first day is meeting cousins I had never known.

Family, yes...

but strangers.

Faces connected by blood, separated by years.

They hugged us, welcomed us, spoke quickly.

But my mind was still somewhere in the Dominican Republic, still trying to understand that Cuenda was no longer home in the way it had been.

The next day was Thanksgiving.

And I didn't even know what Thanksgiving meant.

In the Dominican Republic, we didn't have that holiday.

But in Brooklyn, Thanksgiving was everywhere.

Family gathered at my aunt's house for dinner.

The house was full.

Voices, laughter, English mixed with Spanish, plates moving from hand to hand.

Everyone seemed comfortable.

Everyone seemed to belong.

And then there was us.

The new arrivals.

Still shaken.

Still grieving quietly.

I remember sitting in the corner, feeling like an outcast.

Not because anyone was cruel...

but because our hearts were still back home.

We had left people behind.

We had left a life behind.

But then my eyes drifted to the table.

So much food.

So many snacks.

So much abundance.

In Cuenda, food was measured. Planned. Never overflowing.

Here, the table looked endless.

Platters of things I had never seen.

Desserts. Chips. Sodas.

More than I could understand.

It wasn't just a meal.

It was my first real picture of America.

Within that same week, my aunts and uncles helped my parents look for schools.

Everything moved quickly.

America did not wait for you to catch your breath.

My first school was P.S. 94, only two blocks away from my uncle's house in Sunset Park.

At first, my father would drop me off.

I remember him learning the streets quickly, learning the city for his children.

Then he found work.

And soon, I had to learn how to go on my own.

There was snow.

So much snow.

My clothes were not right.

My body was not used to it.

And my classmates...

they spoke English.

All of them.

I remember sitting in class feeling like my voice had been taken away.

I couldn't express myself.

I couldn't joke.

I couldn't defend myself.

I couldn't belong.

I hated it.

Not because I hated learning...

but because I hated feeling small.

It took time.

Eventually, I found other kids who spoke Spanish.

Kids like me.

Kids carrying two worlds inside them.

Slowly, I began saying little words in English.

A phrase here.

A sentence there.

Until one day, I could hold a conversation.

But even then, my accent stayed with me like evidence.

It made me shy.

Sometimes it made me silent.

I was afraid people would laugh.

Afraid I would sound wrong.

Sunset Park school was rough.

But time does what it always does.

It shapes you.

And slowly...

I started shaping back.

Chapter 7 — Finding My Voice

When you arrive in a new country as a child, people think the hardest part is learning the language.

But the hardest part is learning who you are while you're learning everything else.

In the beginning, I felt like I lived inside silence.

Not because I didn't have thoughts...

but because I didn't have the words.

English surrounded me everywhere — in classrooms, on the streets, on television, in the voices of teachers and children who spoke effortlessly while I struggled just to understand a sentence.

I remember hearing laughter and not knowing what was funny.

I remember wanting to join conversations and feeling like my mouth couldn't keep up with my mind.

I remember going home exhausted, not from schoolwork, but from translation.

From trying.

From surviving.

Sometimes I didn't want to speak at all.

Because speaking meant revealing my accent.

And my accent felt like a spotlight.

It felt like proof that I was different.

I was afraid of being laughed at.

Afraid of saying something wrong.

Afraid of being the immigrant kid forever.

So I stayed quiet more than I should have.

But life doesn't let you stay quiet forever.

Slowly, things changed.

I began making friends — other kids who spoke Spanish, other kids whose families were also trying to build new lives. There was comfort in hearing familiar words in unfamiliar hallways.

There was comfort in knowing I wasn't alone.

Sunset Park was diverse, full of people from everywhere, and that mattered. The neighborhood held many Latinos, many immigrant families, many stories like mine.

And in that community, I started to breathe.

I started to belong.

English came gradually.

A word here.

A sentence there.

Little victories that felt enormous.

I still remember the first time I understood a teacher without needing someone to translate.

The first time I answered a question in English.

The first time I laughed at a joke at the same time as everyone else.

Those moments were small...

but they were everything.

I was building a new self.

And with every new word, confidence grew.

By the time I reached junior high school, something inside me had shifted.

I wasn't just surviving school anymore.

I was participating.

By seventh grade, I felt more accustomed to life in New York.

The city didn't feel like an enemy.

It felt like a challenge I was learning to meet.

I started to enjoy school.

I started to feel known by teachers.

And slowly, the boy from Cuenda was becoming something else too.

A New Yorker.

But even as I adjusted, Cuenda never left me.

I carried it quietly, like a second heartbeat.

The campo.

The river.

The smell of earth after rain.

The sound of neighbors gathered around one television.

The long walks to school with notebooks in hand.

Those memories stayed inside me, reminding me where I began.

By eighth grade, my English was way better.

My confidence was stronger.

I was no longer the silent kid in the corner.

I was just another Latino boy in America.

And during my last year of junior high school, I became something I never imagined when I first arrived:

I became a popular kid.

A smart kid.

I kept honor roll in almost every subject.

Teachers knew me.

Respected me.

Expected good things from me.

That recognition mattered.

It made me feel like I wasn't invisible anymore.

And then baseball entered my life in a serious way.

I was short, but I had a growing passion for the game.

Something about baseball spoke to me.

The discipline.

The teamwork.

The way effort mattered more than where you came from.

Baseball didn't care about your accent.

It cared about your heart.

My junior high coach saw something in me.

By the time I graduated, he had already spoken for me in high school.

He believed in me before I fully believed in myself.

And that belief...

that belief helped shape what came next.

Because the next step was high school.

And in high school, baseball would become more than a sport.

It would become belonging.

It would become brotherhood.

It would become the place where friendships turned into lifelong bonds.

The place where I truly felt, for the first time:

I am here.

I am part of this.

I belong.

Chapter 8 — Brotherhood on the Field

High school felt like a bigger world.

The building was larger, the hallways louder, the expectations heavier. Junior high had been a place where I found my footing again, where my English improved, where I stopped feeling like a stranger.

But high school was different.

High school was where you began to understand that life was moving forward whether you were ready or not.

Still, the transition was easier because many of my friends were coming with me. Familiar faces in a new environment can feel like anchors. It meant I wasn't walking into the unknown completely alone.

And there was another gift waiting for me.

I found old friends from fifth grade — kids I hadn't seen in years.

The moment we saw each other, it was automatic.

We bonded again like no time had passed.

That's one of the strange things about growing up in a neighborhood like Sunset Park. People's lives intersect, separate, then cross again.

Brooklyn has a way of bringing you back to people.

But the real turning point came when I saw the notice posted on the wall:

Baseball tryouts. Practice coming soon.

My heart jumped.

I had played as a kid in Cuenda, running through dust and imagination, swinging makeshift bats in open fields.

Now baseball was here again...

but this time it was real.

Organized.

Structured.

A chance.

Something in me knew I had to go.

So I showed up.

Tryouts are a strange kind of pressure.

You're young, pretending you don't care too much, but inside you care about everything.

Every swing feels like it matters.

Every catch feels like judgment.

Every moment is an audition not only for a team...

but for belonging.

I remember standing there, short kid, quiet determination, wanting so badly to make it.

And then it happened.

I made the team.

That moment was bigger than sports.

It was bigger than a roster.

It was the feeling of being chosen.

Baseball became life-changing for me.

It gave me what every young person needs, especially an immigrant kid trying to find his place:

It gave me belonging.

Suddenly, I had a reason after school.

A place to be.

A jersey that meant something.

A group of boys who became more than teammates.

They became brothers.

Practice after practice, game after game, we built
something that went beyond the field.

We laughed together.

We struggled together.

We won together.

We lost together.

And through all of it, we grew.

Some of the friends I made through baseball are still in
my life today.

Lifelong friendships, born under stadium lights and
Brooklyn skies.

Baseball gave me an identity.

Not the Dominican kid.

Not the immigrant kid.

Not the kid with the accent.

Just a player.

Just part of something.

For the first time, I wasn't just surviving America.

I was living in it.

High school passed the way it always does — faster than you think it will while you're in it.

There were classes, friendships, growing pains, laughter, responsibility slowly creeping in.

And then graduation came.

That moment when you stand at the edge of adulthood and realize childhood is officially behind you.

I decided to leave New York City for college upstate.

Part of me wanted the experience I had seen on television, the independence, the chance to live a different life for a while.

It was exciting...

but it was also frightening.

Leaving home for the first time is always hard.

Leaving a city that had finally begun to feel like mine made it even harder.

But once again, life reminded me that I wasn't alone.

One of my baseball friends decided to join me.

And suddenly, the unknown felt manageable.

We visited the school together.

We looked at apartments together.

We imagined college life together.

It gave me comfort — a sense that I wasn't walking into a new world completely by myself.

It was the perfect bridge between the boy I had been...

and the man I was about to become.

Because I didn't know it yet...

but my life was about to change in the biggest way possible.

Chapter 9 — Upstate Dreams

When I left Brooklyn for college upstate, I carried every emotion a young man can carry at once.

Freedom.

Loneliness.

Excitement.

Fear.

All of it.

I had dreamed of college life the way many kids do — through television, through stories, through imagination. Dorms, independence, new friends, a fresh start.

And now it was real.

I was leaving the neighborhood that had raised me, leaving my parents' home, leaving the city that had finally begun to feel like mine.

The first days felt almost unreal.

There was excitement in the air — the feeling that something was beginning, that I was stepping into my future.

I walked around campus with wide eyes.

New buildings.

New faces.

New energy.

It felt like freedom.

But then night came.

And when things got quiet, loneliness arrived.

Home had always been full — siblings, family voices, the comfort of familiarity. Even in the chaos of growing up in a large family, there was always presence.

Now, for the first time in my life, I was truly on my own.

No parents in the next room.

No childhood safety.

Just me, in an unfamiliar place, trying to act like I knew what I was doing.

I wasn't just a kid from Sunset Park anymore.

I was a young man expected to build something.

And I wanted to.

I wanted the experience. I wanted the independence. I wanted the American dream I had seen from a distance for so long.

But reality came with weight.

Living on my own was expensive.

Life didn't pause just because you were a student.

Bills existed.

Food cost money.

Responsibility followed you everywhere.

So I found a job at a call center.

After classes, I worked evenings, weekends, late-night shifts. Sometimes I would come home exhausted, my mind split between assignments and survival.

The work wasn't glamorous.

But it was honest.

It made me feel like I was earning my way forward.

And then there was the other side of college...

The roommates.

The parties.

The nights that felt carefree.

I was young.

I had friends.

For the first time, there was freedom that didn't exist in my parents' home.

We went out regularly, laughing, living fast, believing we had all the time in the world.

Some nights were fun.

Some nights were reckless.

And some nights, looking back, were just distractions from pressure I didn't yet know how to name.

That's when I met her.

A girl who lived on the same block. It started casually.

Two young people sharing time, attention, and attraction.

Nothing felt heavy at first.

It felt like part of growing up.

Until one day it wasn't.

When she told me she was pregnant, everything slowed down.

I still remember the feeling.

The world didn't end...

but the world I thought I was living in disappeared.

I was in my first semester of college.

Nineteen years old. And suddenly...

I was about to be a father.

Fear doesn't always look like panic.

Sometimes it looks like silence.

I didn't tell my parents right away.

I carried it alone for months, not because I didn't love them, but because I didn't know how to explain that the future they worked so hard to give me was changing before I had even begun.

I waited until she was about five months pregnant before I finally told them.

I can still feel the weight of that moment.

The disappointment I feared.

The responsibility I could not avoid.

The truth that there was no turning back.

Then Carina was born.

Holding her rewired something inside me.

One moment I was a teenager dreaming of college life...

and the next moment I was a father holding a life that depended on me completely.

Fear became clarity.

Responsibility became my identity.

Carina's mother and I moved into a small apartment.

I kept working.

I kept trying to stay in school.

I tried to balance being a young man, a student, and now a father.

But life started getting harder.

Bills. Stress. Sleepless nights.

The pressure of responsibility growing faster than opportunity.

Eventually, we made a decision that felt like surrender, but was really survival.

We moved back to New York City.

Back to my family.

Back to my parents' basement.

It wasn't the life I imagined when I left for college...

but it was the life I needed in order to keep going.

Because the truth was simple:

I had a daughter now.

And somehow...

I had to figure it out.

Chapter 10 — A Father at Nineteen

Moving back to New York City was not easy.

It felt like going backward.

I had left home chasing independence, chasing the college life I imagined, chasing a future I wanted to build.

And now I was back in my parents' basement, a nineteen-year-old father trying to survive.

But pride didn't matter anymore.

Only responsibility did.

Carina was here.

Life depended on me.

We lived in my parents' basement at first.

It wasn't glamorous.

It wasn't what I pictured for myself.

But it was shelter.

It was family.

It was survival.

Eventually, we moved into an apartment and tried again. I found work at another call center, working long hours, trying to create stability.

Then that job closed too.

It felt like life kept pulling the rug out from under me.

So I looked elsewhere.

I found an opportunity with an airline.

I became a flight attendant.

People hear that job title and imagine glamour — travel, destinations, freedom.

But the truth was different.

It was exhausting schedules.

It was missing holidays.

It was long hours on your feet.

It was being away from home when you wanted to be present.

Still, it was work.

It paid the bills.

And I was doing what I had always done...

figuring it out.

Carina's mother worked at a bank near the house.

On the surface, we looked like a young family doing our best.

But beneath the surface, something was already breaking.

I didn't see it clearly at first.

Life was busy.

Survival takes all your attention.

Then came the night that changed everything.

I remember coming home from a trip.

The kind of return where you expect peace — your home, your child, some quiet.

Instead, I walked into something that didn't feel right.

I learned that she had left our daughter — barely one year old — with my best friend.

So she could go out.

Not with friends.

Not with family.

With a man she had met at the bank.

And she didn't come home that night.

Hours passed.

No call.

No explanation.

Then...

she sent me pictures.

Pictures of where she was.

Smiling.

As if I was supposed to accept it.

As if there was no baby at home.

No partner.

No life waiting.

No remorse.

I don't know how to describe that feeling.

It wasn't just betrayal.

It was disrespect so cold it almost felt unreal.

That night, something inside me went still.

Not rage.

Not chaos.

Just clarity.

The next morning, I made the decision.

I sent her out of my life.

There was no screaming.

No negotiation.

No dragging it out.

I knew in my bones that I could not raise my daughter inside that kind of instability.

I could not build a life on betrayal.

So it ended.

She left.

And she took Carina with her.

That was the part that destroyed me.

Not losing her...

losing my child.

One day, I was a father coming home from work.

The next day, my daughter was gone.

Suddenly, fatherhood became something I had to fight for.

At first, it was a four-hour drive each way just to see Carina.

Four hours of road to hold my daughter.

Four hours of road to remind her I existed.

Four hours back.

Every mile felt like punishment.

Later, when she was older — two or three — I began flying to pick her up.

A forty-five-minute flight.

Shorter in time...

heavier in emotion.

Airports became emotional crossroads — joy when I saw her, pain every time I had to let her go again.

Every goodbye felt unnatural.

A father is not built to be distant from his child.

But I kept showing up.

Always.

Then one day, my phone rang.

It was Carina's grandmother.

Her voice was worried.

She told me Carina had been staying with her for two weeks.

Her mother hadn't returned.

She didn't know where she was.

My stomach dropped.

I didn't hesitate.

I got on a flight.

I went to get my daughter.

For a while, Carina was with me.

I already had what felt like custody in practice.

I was raising her.

Building routines.

Creating stability.

I wasn't trying to erase her mother.

I wanted Carina to know both parents.

So when the time came, I agreed to let Carina go on vacation to visit her mother.

I thought it would be good.

Normal.

The right thing.

Then the call came.

Her mother told me Carina would not be returning.

That she was going to stay with her again.

Just like that.

Fear hit me in a way I will never forget.

Not fear for myself.

Fear of losing my daughter again.

That was the moment I realized love alone wasn't enough.

I needed protection.

I needed stability written in ink.

So I went to court.

Court is a strange place to talk about love.

It reduces your life into schedules and statements.

But I walked in there knowing what I was fighting for:

Not control.

Not revenge.

Consistency.

And something happened that I didn't expect.

Carina's mother told the truth.

She said I was a good father.

And that all she wanted was time with her daughter —
vacations, certain weekends, moments that still
mattered.

The court granted me custody, with an agreement that her
mother would still be able to see her.

That was exactly what I wanted.

Because my goal was never to separate.

My goal was to protect my daughter's home.

Her stability.

Her life.

That was the beginning of my true journey as a single father.

It was me and her against the world.

And I promised myself...

Daddy would figure it out.

Chapter 11 — Just Her and Me

After the court granted me custody, life didn't suddenly become easier.

It became clearer.

Carina was with me.

And that meant every day was mine to carry — not halfway, not occasionally, but fully.

I was a single father to a little girl while working as a flight attendant, a job built around leaving.

The irony wasn't lost on me.

My life depended on being away.

But my heart depended on being home.

There were no shortcuts.

Every morning, I would wake up before the day truly began.

The apartment was still quiet, the city outside still asleep.

And there I was — a young father, moving carefully through routine.

I got Carina ready for school, tying her small shoes, making sure her backpack was packed, making sure she had what she needed.

Then I would drop her off like any other parent, smiling as if I wasn't exhausted.

Smiling as if my heart wasn't constantly balancing love and worry.

Every afternoon, I picked her up and spent the day with her.

Those hours were everything.

Simple moments.

Cartoons.

Homework.

Meals.

Little conversations that seemed ordinary but were building something permanent.

And then at night, when other families were settling in, my second shift began.

I would leave her with my sister so I could go to work.

I leaned on my family in the way you have to when you're doing something bigger than yourself.

My siblings, my parents — my whole foundation helped me hold life together.

I would come home late, sometimes barely sleeping, just in time to start the routine again.

It was a cycle of love and exhaustion.

A life built on showing up.

Carina was a sweet child.

Bright.

Observant.

Full of personality.

When she was little, she loved Dora the Explorer.

I still remember her sitting in front of the television, completely focused, repeating words, singing along, smiling like the world was simple.

And in those moments, it was.

I wanted her to feel safe.

I wanted her to feel like she had something special, something beautiful, even if life around us had been complicated.

So I built her a princess room.

I made it just for her.

A room that said:

This is your home.

This is your space.

This is yours.

But the funny thing is...

she almost never slept in it.

Night after night, she would crawl out of that room and come to my bed.

Sometimes she wouldn't even say much.

She would just appear quietly, small and warm, her eyes heavy with sleep, and ask softly:

"Daddy... can I sleep with you?"

And of course, I always said yes.

Because what she wanted wasn't the room.

It was comfort.

It was closeness.

It was reassurance.

She didn't need a castle.

She needed her father.

There were two things I always told her.

The first was:

"Me and you against the world."

The second was:

"Daddy will figure it out."

I said it when bills felt heavy.

I said it when schedules didn't make sense.

I said it when I didn't actually know how the next week would work.

Those words weren't magic.

They were commitment.

I didn't always have answers.

But I always had her.

And that was enough.

As the years passed, things shifted.

She became more independent.

She learned her way to school.

The days stopped feeling like constant survival and started feeling like routine.

Eventually, it was just her and me.

A quiet household.

A bond built through years of presence.

Carina grew into a smart, grounded young woman.

Today, she is twenty-four years old — a schoolteacher pursuing her master's degree.

When I look at her, I don't just see my daughter.

I see every mile driven.

Every flight taken.

Every night shift survived.

Every promise kept.

And through all of it, she still carries those words with her.

Me and you against the world.

Daddy will figure it out.

She tells people now, proudly, that somehow her dad always did.

And the truth is...

I didn't always know how.

But I never stopped trying.

Chapter 12 — Grounded

For thirteen years, the airline was my life.

It wasn't just a job.

It was stability.

It was how I paid bills.

It was how I raised my daughter.

It was how I kept moving forward.

Flight after flight.

Schedule after schedule.

Years stacking quietly.

And after a while, you start believing something will last simply because it has lasted so long.

Then one day...

it didn't.

After a flight, I was picked up and taken into an office.

The walk there felt strange.

Quiet.

Like something was wrong before anyone even said a word.

I remember sitting down while my manager looked through paperwork, reviewing my absences with the seriousness of someone searching for a conclusion.

What they didn't understand — what a file can never explain — was that most of those absences weren't about laziness or carelessness.

They were about childcare.

They were days when I didn't have a babysitter.

Days when I had to choose my daughter over a company that didn't know her name.

I was placed on an investigation pending termination.

At that time, my partner was pregnant with our second child.

We were building a family.

Believing we were standing on something firm.

Then the call came.

I was terminated.

Just like that.

Thirteen years reduced to one sentence.

I didn't know how to feel because everything hit me at once.

Disbelief.

Shock.

Fear.

Shame.

It was like my mind couldn't decide which emotion to hold first...

so it held them all.

I remember sitting there afterward, frozen.

Not crying.

Not moving.

Just staring at nothing, trying to understand how quickly something important could be taken away.

I had no savings.

No degree.

No plan.

And now I had an entire family relying on me.

It wasn't just losing a job.

It felt like losing the ground beneath my feet.

Like being dropped into uncertainty with no warning.

Eventually, I went home.

And the hardest part wasn't the termination itself.

The hardest part was telling my partner.

Saying it out loud made it real.

I could see the fear in her eyes.

The questions neither of us could answer yet.

What now?

How do we survive this?

How do I start over...

again?

I applied everywhere.

Interview after interview.

Applications disappearing into silence.

Days filled with waiting.

And in that waiting, pressure grew heavier.

Then I made a decision rooted in humility.

I went to work with my brother.

He owned a small woodworking shop.

There was no ego left in me at that point.

Only the need to provide.

At first, I swept floors.

Moved materials.

Did whatever needed to be done.

Starting over doesn't feel heroic.

It feels like being brought back to the beginning when you thought you were already past that chapter.

But even while doing simple tasks, my mind stayed awake.

I observed everything.

On job sites, I watched the project managers closely —
the way they spoke, the way they organized, the way they
carried authority.

And slowly, something formed inside me.

I realized I had the mechanism for that job.

I could do it.

I wasn't meant to stay sweeping floors forever.

So I started researching.

Studying.

Learning on my own.

I took the New York State General Contractor license
exam.

And I passed.

Becoming licensed wasn't just a certification.

It was a turning point.

A signal that my life was not ending.

It was shifting.

For almost a year, I sat on that license.

The company existed on paper before it existed in reality.

I was hungry.

Restless.

Waiting for the first opportunity.

Then it came.

My first contract — an apartment building in the city.

I needed a team, so I used the same guys my brother trusted.

Standing on that job site for the first time as the contractor felt surreal.

Not because I had "made it."

But because I had rebuilt myself again from nothing.

I had been grounded...

and I rose anyway.

Because that's what I had always done.

That's what my life demanded.

And what my children deserved.

Chapter 13 — Joy After Storms

Life has a strange way of giving you light after darkness.

Not because the struggle disappears...

but because love keeps arriving.

In the middle of rebuilding myself, in the middle of learning a new industry, in the middle of starting over yet again...

I became a father again.

When Martin Jr. was born, it was one of the proudest moments of my life.

My first son.

I don't even know how to explain what it felt like.

Carina made me a father.

But Martin made me a father to a boy.

And something about that hit me differently.

I was the proudest dad imaginable.

I would sleep next to him, stay up late just watching him breathe.

I would wake up in the middle of the night to make sure his chest was still rising and falling.

It was insane.

But it was love.

That overwhelming realization that this tiny human depended on me completely.

I remember thinking:

How is this real?

Then he started talking.

That first "daddda"...

It hits you somewhere deep.

And when he began running toward me, calling me Daddy, it felt like joy given a voice.

I think I bought him a glove and a bat while he wasn't even walking yet.

That's how proud I was.

I was already dreaming of playing catch.

Already imagining passing something down.

Now Martin Jr. is ten years old.

And he's like my little buddy.

He enjoys the same things I do.

He wants to be around me, to learn, to laugh, to share life's small adventures.

Katie came after.

She is nine now, full of personality, full of energy, competitive in the best way.

She brings laughter into every room.

And then Mateo.

Mateo is three.

The youngest.

Wild with life.

The kind of child who doesn't understand danger because everything still feels like possibility.

Together, they make my world loud, messy, beautiful.

Martin Jr., Katie, and I have our traditions.

We go fishing together.

And it always becomes a competition.

They fight over who catches the biggest fish.

Who gets the first bite.

Who is the better fisherman.

Those moments are everything.

Simple...

ordinary...

but priceless.

We don't bring Mateo.

The first time we brought him fishing, he wanted to jump into the ocean yelling that it was a pool.

That was the end of that.

Mateo is banned from fishing for now.

Carina doesn't like fishing much either.

Not because she doesn't love being with us...

but because the last time she came she spent the whole day running after Mateo instead of relaxing.

That's family life.

Beautiful chaos.

Fatherhood has not been one story for me.

It has been many stories.

Carina, my firstborn, who taught me responsibility.

Martin Jr., my son, who brought a new kind of pride.

Katie, who fills the world with laughter and fire.

Mateo, the wild little one, still too young to understand danger but already full of life.

Each of them has shaped me.

Each of them has given me a reason to keep showing up.

Chapter 14— The Hardest Goodbyes

My second long-term relationship eventually came to an end when Mateo was three years old.

It's not easy to write that sentence, even now.

Because endings are never just endings.

They are wounds.

They are adjustments.

They are moments where you realize life is changing again, whether you are ready or not.

Things between us were not going well.

The tension became constant.

The disagreements grew heavier.

And when it ended, it ended badly — not in a dramatic way, but in the painful way that leaves silence behind.

I had thought about separation before it happened.

And even thinking about it hurt.

Not because of pride.

Not because of ego.

But because of the children.

The thought of being apart from them felt unbearable.

I remembered what it was like when Carina was young — distance, uncertainty, the fear of losing time you can never get back.

I didn't want that again.

I wanted better.

I wanted my kids to grow up knowing their father was present.

I wanted them to look up during a game, a school activity, a family gathering...

and see me there.

And they do.

That has always mattered to me more than anything.

Their mother moved into an apartment in the city, closer to her job and closer to good schools for the kids.

We agreed I would help with bills and child support.

And that I would have the kids every other weekend.

It wasn't the life I imagined.

But it was the life I accepted, because fatherhood does not end with separation.

Fatherhood is not about convenience.

It is about commitment.

The hardest part wasn't the schedule.

The hardest part was the goodbye.

The dropping off.

The moment the door closes and the house becomes quiet again.

There were days when I would bring the kids back to their mother...

and Martin Jr. would hug me the way only a child can.

A tight, tight hug.

The kind that isn't casual.

The kind that holds on.

Then he would look down, his voice suddenly softer, almost fragile, and he would say:

"Goodbye, Dad."

Something about the way he lowered his head made it hurt even more.

I never forgot it.

I would ask him, "Are you okay?"

And he would always say yes.

But fathers know.

We feel what our children cannot fully say.

One day, after I dropped him off, my phone rang almost immediately.

It was Martin.

His voice was small.

And he said he missed me.

He said he wanted to be with me.

I don't even remember what I answered.

I just remember driving home with tears that wouldn't stop.

I cried the entire ride.

Because separation is hard in ways I still can't properly describe.

I live for my children.

And not having them near me all the time has been one of the deepest adjustments of my life.

The apartment is quiet in a way that doesn't feel peaceful.

It feels unfinished.

But life doesn't ask your permission.

It teaches you to adjust.

So I have learned.

I have adapted.

I have focused on what I can control:

Being present whenever I have them.

Making every weekend count.

Making Sunday dinners sacred.

Showing up at games, at school events, at moments that matter.

Reminding them again and again that even if we live in different homes...

they never live far from my love.

Sometimes fatherhood is not about being perfect.

Sometimes it is simply about refusing to disappear.

And I have never disappeared.

Chapter 15 — Legacy

Even after separation, even after change, even after life rearranged itself again...

I am still here.

I live alone now, in an apartment full of memories.

Quiet when the kids aren't there.

Alive when they are.

Every time they walk through the door, it becomes home again.

This past Christmas, I took them on vacation.

But this time, the trip wasn't just about getting away.

It was about going back.

I brought Martin and Katie to the Dominican Republic — back to my home, back to the soil that raised me, back to Cuenda.

They were excited in a way that surprised me. They didn't see it as a simple vacation. They saw it as something meaningful, something personal.

They wanted to understand where their father came from.

And once we arrived, Cuenda captured them completely.

Of all the places we visited, that small campo was all they wanted. They didn't care about big cities or tourist spots. They wanted the dirt roads, the open air, the simplicity.

They wanted Cuenda.

Martin found a friend there — a boy named Michael.

What made it even funnier was that Michael didn't speak English, and Martin spoke only a little Spanish.

And yet somehow... they understood each other perfectly.

They laughed.

They played.

They ran through the same kind of space I once ran through as a child.

I watched them from a distance, quietly smiling to myself, thinking about my own days growing up there — barefoot, carefree, surrounded by life in its simplest form.

Seeing my son playing in Cuenda brought me a joy I can't fully explain.

It felt like time folding in on itself.

Like life was giving me a moment of peace.

A moment that said:

Look how far you've come.

Look what you've built.

Watching them laugh, explore, and spend time with me and my family reminded me of something simple:

Presence is everything.

They had a blast.

And so did I.

Because in those moments, nothing else matters.

Not the stress.

Not the setbacks.

Not the chapters that were hard.

Just the sound of my kids enjoying life.

Just the feeling of being their dad.

When I have them, I make sure we have Sunday dinner.

Every time.

We sit at the table.

We eat.

We talk.

We laugh.

Sometimes those dinners are loud.

Sometimes they are calm.

Sometimes Mateo is trying to turn the whole room into a playground.

But those moments are sacred.

Because one day, they will grow up.

And what will remain are the memories.

Of sitting together.

Of being family.

Of love holding everything in place even when life wasn't perfect.

My family has always been my rock.

Even though I am the youngest of fifteen, I have always been close to my siblings. I come from a large family filled with nieces and nephews that I consider my own.

We are connected in a way that time and distance cannot break.

My parents remain my foundation.

I still go to them for advice, for wisdom, for conversations that remind me where I come from.

They raised me with strength.

They raised me with sacrifice.

They raised me with love.

And I carry that into my own children.

When I look back on my life, I don't see a straight path.

I see a boy from Cuenda walking miles to school, notebooks in hand.

I see a mother walking into the fields carrying food for workers, and a little boy behind her carrying water, trying to keep up.

I see a town gathered around one television powered by a car battery, laughing together in the Dominican night.

I see a child making a mistake with a match, watching everything burn, learning too young how quickly life can change.

I see a nine-year-old arriving in Brooklyn on November 23rd, 1993, feeling winter hit like a brick.

I see the immigrant kid afraid of his accent.

I see the teenager who found belonging through baseball.

I see the nineteen-year-old becoming a father before he understood adulthood.

I see the young dad driving four hours just to hold his daughter.

I see the single father working nights, coming home exhausted, still showing up.

I see Dora the Explorer on the TV, and Carina crawling into my bed because what she needed was not a princess room...

but her father.

I see thirteen years with an airline, and then termination.

I see fear.

Shame.

Starting over.

Sweeping floors.

Then becoming licensed.

Becoming a General Contractor.

Building again from nothing.

I see Martin Jr. running toward me yelling "Daddda."

I see Katie fighting for the biggest fish.

I see Mateo trying to jump into the ocean because he thought it was a pool.

I see the tight hugs at drop-off, the soft goodbyes, the tears driving home.

I see a life full of storms...

and full of love.

This isn't a story about money.

Or titles.

Or perfection.

This is a story about showing up.

About responsibility.

About resilience.

About choosing love even when life is heavy.

It is a story about a father who kept going.

Epilogue — Returning to Cuenda

Sometimes, in my quietest moments, I return to Cuenda.

Not with my feet...

but with my heart.

I see the dirt road again.

The one I walked as a child with notebooks in my hands, heading toward a small wooden schoolhouse in the distance.

I hear the river.

I smell the earth after rain.

I remember the simplicity of life back then — how hard it was, and yet how pure it felt.

There was struggle, yes.

But there was also laughter.

There was family.

There was community.

We didn't have much, but we had each other.

And sometimes, I close my eyes and I can still feel it —
the warmth of the Dominican sun, the sound of neighbors
gathering at night, the joy of baseball played in dust
instead of stadiums.

It amazes me how life can carry you so far from where you
began.

A boy from Cuenda becomes a man in New York City.

A child who didn't speak English becomes a father raising
children in America.

A young immigrant who once felt invisible becomes
someone who has built a life, a family, and a legacy.

When I think about everything I've lived through, I don't
measure it in money.

I measure it in moments.

Holding my daughter Carina when I was nineteen,
realizing life was no longer just mine.

Sitting beside her as a single father, hearing her ask,
"Daddy, can I sleep with you?"

Watching Martin Jr. run toward me yelling "Daddda,"
becoming my little buddy.

Hearing Katie laugh as she fights to catch the biggest fish.

Chasing Mateo as he tries to turn the ocean into a swimming pool.

Feeling my son hug me tight at drop-off, his voice soft as he says goodbye.

These are the things that define my life.

Not titles.

Not jobs.

Not setbacks.

Just love.

Just presence.

Just showing up.

I have started over more times than I ever expected.

I have lost things I thought were permanent.

I have faced fear, shame, heartbreak.

But I have also discovered something powerful:

Life can break you...

and you can still rebuild.

Not because you are unshakable.

But because love makes you willing.

Love makes you fight for tomorrow.

Today, I still carry the same promise I carried when Carina was small:

Me and you against the world.

Daddy will figure it out.

I didn't always know how.

But somehow... I always did.

And now, as I look at my children, I understand something clearly:

Everything was worth it.

Every long night.

Every sacrifice.

Every restart.

Because they are here.

And I am here.

And the story continues.

Somewhere in the quiet of Cuenda, the boy I once was is still walking that road.

And somewhere in New York, the father I have become is still doing the same thing he has always done:

Figuring it out.

One step at a time.

Daddy Will Figure It Out

There are words we say in life that become more than words.

They become anchors.

They become promises.

They become the thing you return to when everything feels uncertain.

For me, those words were simple:

"Daddy will figure it out."

I said them first to my daughter when it was just the two of us.

When the world felt too big.

When bills were heavy.

When schedules didn't make sense.

When life was asking more from me than I thought I could give.

She would look at me with those trusting eyes, and I would say it again:

Daddy will figure it out.

Sometimes I said it for her.

Sometimes I said it for myself.

Because the truth is, fatherhood doesn't come with a manual.

Life doesn't hand you a map.

And yet... somehow, you keep going.

Somehow, you find the next step.

I didn't always have money.

I didn't always have stability.

I didn't always have answers.

But I always had love.

And love makes you resourceful.

Love makes you fight for tomorrow.

Love makes you show up even when you're tired.

Love makes you become the kind of person you didn't know you could be.

People sometimes look at me now and say, "You always figured it out."

And I appreciate that.

But what they don't see is that "figuring it out" isn't magic.

It's waking up anyway.

It's trying anyway.

It's choosing not to quit.

It's carrying fear in one hand and responsibility in the other.

It's being unsure... and still moving forward.

A Final Note to My Children

Carina, Martin Jr., Katie, and Mateo,

If you are reading this one day, I want you to know something clearly:

Everything I did, every sacrifice I made, every time I started over, was for you.

I did not have all the answers when life tested me. I made mistakes. I learned as I went. But I never stopped loving you, and I never stopped trying to be present.

You were never the reason life was hard.

You were the reason I stayed strong.

Carina, you made me a father before I knew what that truly meant. You taught me responsibility, patience, and unconditional love.

Martin Jr., you taught me pride in a way only a son can. Watching you grow, laugh, and become your own person fills me with joy I can't explain.

Katie, you taught me that strength and kindness can live in the same heart. Your laughter lights up every room.

Mateo, you taught me that life never stops being new and exciting. You remind me to stay curious, playful, and present.

No matter where life takes you, always remember where you come from. You come from love. You come from resilience. You come from a family that stood together even when things were not easy.

If you ever feel lost, unsure, or afraid, remember this:

Your father believed in you before you believed in yourself.

And I always will.

A Message for Single Parents

There is something I want to say directly to the single mothers and fathers out there.

To the parents doing it alone.

To the ones carrying silent weight.

To the ones who love their children so deeply it hurts.

I see you.

I know the exhaustion.

The long nights.

The mornings where you wake up with no rest but still have to be strong.

The moments where you sit in your car after a drop-off and breathe through tears before driving away.

The guilt.

The pressure.

The constant feeling that you have to be everything.

Let me tell you something:

Your presence matters more than your perfection.

Your children don't need a flawless parent.

They need a real one.

They need someone who stays.

Someone who tries.

Someone who loves them loudly through actions, not just words.

Some days, survival is the victory.

Some days, getting through the day is enough.

And if no one has told you this...

you are doing something heroic.

Not because it looks heroic.

But because love is heroic when it refuses to disappear.

To the Reader

If you've made it to this page, thank you.

Thank you for sitting with my story.

Thank you for allowing my life to live in your hands for a moment.

If there is one thing I hope you take from these pages, it is this:

You are not alone.

Whatever you are carrying — fear, regret, exhaustion, uncertainty — it does not define the end of your story.

Life is not a straight line.

It bends.

It breaks.

It asks you to begin again.

And that does not mean you failed.

It means you are still alive.

Still trying.

Still moving forward.

If you are a parent, especially a single parent, I hope you see yourself here and feel seen.

If you are an immigrant, I hope you feel pride in how far you've come.

If you are someone who feels behind in life, I hope you remember that progress is not measured by speed, but by perseverance.

Sometimes survival is the victory.

Sometimes love is enough.

Sometimes getting up again is the bravest thing you can do.

And when you don't know what comes next, remember this:

You don't need all the answers.

You just need the courage to take the next step.

Because somehow...

we figure it out.

Acknowledgments

This book exists because of the people who have stood beside me through every chapter of my life.

To my parents — thank you for your sacrifice, your wisdom, and the foundation you gave me.

To my siblings, nieces, and nephews — my family has always been my rock.

To my children — Carina, Martin Jr., Katie, and Mateo — you are the reason behind every step forward.

And to anyone who reads these pages: thank you for allowing my story to live beyond me.

If you see yourself somewhere in these words, know that you are not alone

Final Words

To my children — Carina, Martin Jr., Katie, and Mateo — you have always been my purpose. Everything I built, every restart, every sacrifice was made with you in mind. My love for you is permanent.

And to the reader — if you found yourself in these pages, know this: you are not alone. Life is not a straight line. It bends, it breaks, and sometimes it asks us to begin again.

But beginning again is not failure.

It is courage.

It is hope in action.

Sometimes survival is the victory. Sometimes love is enough. And somehow, even when we don't know how...

we figure it out.

Me and you against the world. Daddy will figure it out.

www.ingramcontent.com/pod-product-compliance
Lightning Source LLC
Chambersburg PA
CBHW030551130626
46552CB00006B/2501